ERIC AND ETHEL:

An Old-Fashioned Fairy Tale.

BY

FRANCIS FRANCIS,

AUTHOR OF "PICKACKIFAX, A NOVEL IN RHYME," "THE REAL SALT,"
"ANGLER'S REGISTER," "NEWTON DOGVANE," "SIDNEY BELLEW,"
"FISH CULTURE," "SPORTING SKETCHES," "A BOOK ON ANGLING,"
"BY LAKE AND RIVER," "ANGLING,"
"HOT POT," "THE PRACTICAL MANAGEMENT OF FISHERIES," ETC. ETC.

LONDON:

SAMPSON LOW, MARSTON, SEARLE, & RIVINGTON

CROWN BUILDINGS, 188 FLEET STREET.

1885.

" The robbers, however, were snoring loudly, and he began to climb as quickly as he could.'—*Page* 83.

PREFACE.

THIS story was written many years ago for my children.

It has become the custom to write for children with what we call "a purpose." The child's book now-a-days is too often like that senna tea which, sweetened until it was fifty times nastier than in its natural state, our dear parents used to tender us under the title of "French coffee," or like those irrelevant spoonfuls of jam offered us with a liberality that aroused suspicion and invoked the question, "What's that queer-looking white stuff in it?"

When I was young children's books did not have purposes, if we except the case of

"Sandford and Merton." And I freely admit that, as a boy, I did not like "Sandford and Merton." I did not believe in it. Master Sandford was the "white stuff" in the jam, and old Barlow was "French coffee;" and I should have enjoyed fighting Tommy Merton in our playground on any Wednesday afternoon, and with equal pleasure would have engaged Master Sandford on the following Saturday.

Actuated by these noble sentiments, I am going back to the old method of pure storytelling; and I warn you, therefore, that if you expect to learn anything from the history of Eric and Ethel, you will be disappointed. It is full of impossibilities. There is not a line of it true. Historically, geographically, geologically, ethnologically, zoologically, entomologically, and genealogically, it is absurd. Nevertheless, it may amuse children, and if it accomplishes this much, it entirely fulfils its object.

FRANCIS FRANCIS.

CONTENTS.

CONTENTS.

ERIC AND ETHEL.

CHAPTER I.

WHICH TELLS WHO WAS WHO, ONCE UPON A TIME.

MANY years ago, so long ago, indeed,
that it was before the greatest great-
grandfather of any one now living
could recollect, in a little village among the
mountains in a distant part of Norway, there
lived one Hans the herdsman. A hard-work-
ing, hard-living, hard-featured, hard-a-weather
sort of fellow was Hans—the sort of fellow
one likes to meet trudging through the snow
on a frosty morning, with a short pipe in his

A

mouth, a blue nose, a cheery blue eye, and a
merry smile, saying as plainly as eye or smile
can say, "God save you kindly, friend!" to
every passer-by. Hans was one of the herds-
men of the great Prince of Greatswello, whom
he had never seen; for the business that had
to be transacted with himself and his neighbours was done by a steward, who visited
them once a year, and a very tough and
exacting customer they found him.

Hans had a wife, a thrifty, cleanly, comely
woman, who kept both his cottage and himself
in rare order; and they had one son, the little
Eric; but although Mrs. Hans longed for a
daughter, and had made offerings to all the
saints in the Calendar to induce them to bestow
one upon her, they had no other children.
Hans was very fond of Eric, and when he
went forth to tend his goats and reindeer,
would take him with him, and sitting down
in some snug corner behind a rock or cairn,
with the child wrapped in a warm sheepskin,

would teach him to carve curious faces on knotty sticks and make bottle-puzzles or puzzles in bottles, the introduction there of which the beholder found quite as much diffi- culty in explaining as subsequently George III. found in understanding how the apples got inside the dumplings. Besides these accom- plishments he taught him many more useful arts; and, tired of instruction, would tell him stories of fairies, and point out to him the Troll- mounds—little knolls, like large overgrown ant or mole hills, which the Trolls were said to inhabit. He would recount to him their mar- vellous feats, and those of the other inhabitants of Elf-land, relating how ill-luck had befallen the flocks of a certain herdsman who hung a bell upon the neck of one of his goats (it being well known that the Trolls disliked the sound of bells); how such and such a little maiden had been decoyed away by mischievous elfs, and had never since been seen; and how the healthy child of a neighbour had been changed in the cradle for a peevish little imp, that was always performing spiteful tricks, and finally, in the eleventh year of its mortal existence, disappeared altogether. He would tell him how, by placing beer and cakes out of doors, he might obtain the good offices of the Niss (whom he himself had once seen sitting up in a large birch-tree in front of their cottage, and whose patronage he had secured by promising never to fell the tree), and would paint some of the pranks played in his time by Loki, the patron of thieves. And then, with bated breath, he would speak of the Midgard serpent, that encircles the world, and of the huge Kraaken that lives deep down below the Maelström, and swallows up ships as we do sugar-plums; and perhaps he would even mention the Grimm, who dwelt in a pool under a deep foaming waterfall near them, and who, if he chose, could teach any one who made proper offerings to him to excel in the most extraordinary manner in music. Hans, knowing no better, believed in all the queer things he told his son; and he, as all good little boys should do, believed his father. He put out the best cakes and ale for the Niss therefore, and was careful not to annoy the Trolls, and altogether conducted himself in such a way that he obtained quite a good character in Elf-land. But, besides all this legendary lore, he learnt to read and write (rare accomplishments in those days); and his mother, a most superior woman for her station, taught him what is the inspiration of all true politeness, namely, to be considerate and unselfish to everybody. This poor herdsman's son, therefore, had manners which would have become a gentleman. He learnt also to play upon a little pipe which Hans made for him, and taught his dog Tray to stand upon his hind legs, and dance to his music. Poor, honest, rough old Tray, an odd figure he looked, I can tell you, performing in this fashion!

Now not far from Hans's cottage there lived

a miller, by name Jan Beanflaverem. This miller, Jan, was a wealthy man, but not at all a good one. In order to increase his profits he adulterated his flour with ground bark of trees, dried bones, and other nasty things. Many of his successors crossed the sea, I am told, and set up as millers in this country; but if ever they are caught playing any of Jan's tricks here, I hope they will be made to eat ground bark and bones themselves, and be deprived of all their profits.

Jan was a fine portly fellow, who did not look as if he cheated, but unfortunately you cannot always tell a person's character by his looks. When he stood at the door of his mill in his skin doublet, with his gold watch-chain and seals hanging from his pocket, and smoked his long birch-wood pipe, he seemed a man of no slight importance. And when the people came from far and near, bringing sacks of corn to be ground, and Jan measured out the flour and meal with his big thumb thrust into the

measure (another cheating way of his), he *was*
a man of no slight importance; for there was
not another mill within ten miles of his, so he
had things all his own way, and did as he
pleased.

Now this pompous, cheating, wealthy Jan
had one little girl, the fairest, prettiest, and
most amiable little maid ever seen anywhere.
She was slim and fairy-like, with the longest
golden curls flowing down on her trim shoulders,
with a beautiful white skin, cheeks like a rose,
and blue eyes, so soft, so kind, and pitying
that everybody loved her.   Her little feet
were so small that she could hardly keep her
shoes on them, and round her tiny waist she
always had a broad blue or pink sash with
a big bow in the middle of it.   About her
birth there was a mystery, for Jan had never
been married.   To tell the truth, she was not
really his daughter, but belonged to some one
else, as you will learn by-and-by.   She had
come into Jan's possession once when there

were heavy floods throughout the country, and it was rumoured that jewels and lace had been found upon her; but whether this were true, or how she had first been discovered, no one but the miller himself knew exactly; and as he was not the man to talk about his affairs, curiosity on the subject had died out.

Jan as nearly loved little Ethel as he was capable of loving anything. He once gave her a shilling to play with, but it was a bad one that he had accidentally taken at market after drinking more than was good for him; and shortly afterwards, a poor old woman requiring change, he took it away again and passed it off to her. Oh, he was a wicked old scamp! And cheating never prospers, as you will see in the end.

Eric, who was about three years older than Ethel, often saw her picking wild-flowers in the mill-meadows, and becoming in course of time friendly with her, taught her to make the flowers into nosegays and garlands. He

climbed trees to pick nuts for her, brought
her the ripest and sweetest cranberries, and
tamed a little goat to draw a sledge he made
for her in the winter. Though he gladly did
anything he could do to oblige anybody, there
was nothing he liked nearly as well as ren-
dering Ethel a service, so that they grew
eventually to be quite fond of one another,
and all their play-hours were spent together.
Jan Beanflaverem troubled himself little about
her education, and had not Eric taught her
to read and write, and told her what was
proper and good, and what was not so, she
would have grown up wilful and ignorant.
Being, however, naturally amiable and quick,
and being anxious, moreover, to please her
playmate, she profited greatly by his instruction.

This went on for some time, and since it
saved Jan some expense (not that he would
have put himself to any *great* expense for
anybody), he ignored their friendship. One

day, however, something occurred to put him out of temper with Hans, and as it was his nature, when unable to revenge himself upon whoever had irritated him, to vex some one related to them, he indulged his spite against Eric. Seeing the children seated under a bower of osiers (which Eric had made for Ethel), where the herdsman's son was reading a story-book aloud, and the little girl playing with a kitten he had given her, Jan took his way towards them.

"Halloo!" cried he in a loud, rough way; "halloo, what's this? My daughter playing with a little vagabond!"

"He isn't a vagabond, father, please, he's Eric," said the poor little maid, trembling for her companion.

"How dare you contradict me, Miss? I say he is a vagabond, and I won't have him here, teaching you to contradict your father. And what's all this?—stealing my osiers to make hiding-places! I'll soon settle all that

"And snatching poor little kit roughly out of Ethel's arms, he swung her over the hedge, and right into the middle of the mill-dam."—*Page* 12.

sort of thing!" and he pulled up the osiers, scattering them far and wide, and quite destroying the bower. "What's that you've got there too?—a cat!"

"O father, please, please don't hurt Kitty!" exclaimed Ethel, clasping her favourite in her arms.

"Where did you get it?"

Seeing that Ethel was silent, Eric spoke up. "Please, Mr. Beanflaverem, I gave it to her; it's one of our Tib's kittens; and she is such a famous mouser that I thought you would let Ethel keep her; she will catch all the mice in the mill."

"Oh, she will, will she! We'll see. I·am not going to have any lazy cats drinking up the milk and eating the meal in my mill. Hand her here!" And snatching poor little kit roughly out of Ethel's arms, he swung her over the hedge, and right into the middle of the mill-dam. Then seizing Ethel's hand, as she burst into a flood of tears at the shocking fate of her pet, he dragged her towards the mill, threatening Eric with "a thick stick about his shoulders if he caught him on his premises again."

No sooner was he gone than, jumping the hedge and running into the water (luckily not deep just there), Eric recovered the poor kitten, which was almost drowned; and drying her as well as possible, put her under his jacket and hastened home. He too would have cried at seeing the treatment Ethel and her pet had received, only he was so angry that he wished he had been big enough to punch old Jan Beanflaverem's head, and resolved when he was older to do so.

CHAPTER II.

WHAT THE NISS SAID—THE LOSS OF ETHEL—WHAT ERIC DID AFTER THAT—AND WHAT THE NISS DID AFTER THAT AGAIN.

AFTER a while things, so far as the children were concerned, resumed their usual course, for, their intimacy presenting many advantages to Jan, he winked at it, and in a gruff, disagreeable way, was even civil to Eric when he met him alone.

One afternoon Eric was going out to join his father and assist him in driving home the goats, when he suddenly recollected that it was Thursday, and bethought him that he might not be home in time to put out cakes and ale for the Niss. Selecting, therefore, the biggest and brownest cake he could find, he cut a large hole in the middle of it, and filled it with the brightest virgin honey, and drawing a mug of sparkling spruce beer, placed them both on a stone at the foot of the Niss's birch-tree. Returning past the tree, after having fetched his dog Tray to accompany him, he was greatly surprised to see that the cake and beer had disappeared. It was very unusual for this to occur so soon; but the honey was singularly fragrant, and the Niss, being hungry, could not resist its temptation. As Eric went by he heard the queerest little sneeze imaginable above him.

"Ak yaffo, yaffo!" Tray growled and looked startled. "Ak yaffo, yaffo!"

Whence could it come? Certainly from somewhere in the tree, and looking aloft Eric saw, crouched in a moss-lined hole formed by the dismemberment some years ago of a large branch, the oddest little figure imaginable. It was the Niss. Even had he not

been munching the identical cake and drinking the beer provided for him a few minutes
before, Eric would have recognised him immediately by his red cap and grey worsted dress.
He nodded rapidly to the young herdsman,
who stood hat in hand, respectfully waiting for
him to speak; but, with every appearance of
enjoyment, he continued to eat in silence, nodding between each mouthful. At length, having swallowed the last morsel of cake, finished
the beer, looked into the bottom of the mug,
and even held it upside down to see that there
was not a drop left in it, he licked his fingers
slowly with his long hairy tongue, scanned his
thumbs to see that not the smallest particle
of honey escaped him, and putting the mug
under his arm, turned about and came down
the tree like a monkey. Such an odd little
chap was he to look at that some folks might
have felt inclined to laugh at him; but they
would not have been guilty twice of doing
so, for the Niss objects to be ridiculed, and

usually takes vengeance in a most summary manner upon any one who thus offends him. Eric knew this.

"I hope, sir, that you found the cake to your liking?" he observed deferentially.

"Capital!" replied the Niss, "capital! That is first-rate honey of your mother's, Eric— first-rate! I'll give her bees a good turn, a famous turn, next year. Let me see. She shall have a swarm on the 1st May. I was very fond of your mother when she was a girl, Eric; indeed, she narrowly escaped being Mrs. Niss, and I have always taken an interest in the family since."

"Thank you, sir; I'm sure we're very grateful."

"I know you are," said the little man, pulling up his long grey hose, and sitting down on a stone. "And the cake, Eric, was done to a turn. She is a notable woman, your mother."

At this juncture that faithful but indiscreet

"'I know you are,' said the little man, pulling up his long grey hose, and sitting down on a stone."—*Page 17*.

animal, Tray, roused the Niss's indignation by snapping at his calf, or rather at that part of his spindle shank which passed for it. Lifting his leg he gave the dog a slight kick, which caused him to fly up in the air, and after describing a parabola over a neighbouring cow-shed, alighted in a prickly bush on the other side of it, whence, disengaging himself, he darted away, howling "Pen and ink!" dreadfully.

"Humph!" chuckled the Niss, "grief has driven him away, at anyrate, and that's a comfort. Give him to the miller, Eric, as a great favour; and when old Jan is standing by I will nip Tray's tail, and as he will be unable to see me, he will bite Jan. Ha! ha! ha! That will be sport! And then the miller will drown him; and then thieves will come and steal his money; and so everybody will be served rightly, and we shall all be comfortable."

Eric did not like to give Tray away; still

less did he approve the fate proposed for him; and, aware of the struggle in his mind, the Niss watched his face keenly. Come what might, however, Eric determined not to offend the Niss, so at length he replied simply, "I will do as you wish, sir; you shall not be annoyed any more, if I can help it."

The Niss looked very pleased at this, and patting the boy's head with the heel of his boot in a most patronising manner, said, "Good lad! good lad! You will be a great man one of these days, Eric; I have planned it all."

Seeing the dwarf glance a little sadly at the empty mug, Eric hastened to say, "It is very hot to-day, sir; might I venture to offer your worship another draught of spruce?"

"You might venture, my son, for"—(smacking his lips with a sound like a pistol-shot) —"it's capital spruce, and the weather *is* hot. You're a lad of discrimination, Eric."

Eric fetched another mug of beer, which the Niss disposed of at his leisure, and then slapping his thigh and cocking his arm in a military fashion, he became highly conversational.

"About that miller, now, Eric," he said, after he had talked for a little, "about him and his daughter. She is a great deal too good for him."

"Is she, sir?" rejoined Eric.

"*Isn't* she, sir?" retorted the Niss sharply; "don't you know she is? Why ask stupid questions? Is not she a nice, pretty, little thing? and is not he a great, vulgar brute, with no more feeling or manners than a bull-frog? Is not she charitable and humane, and he stingy and hard-hearted? Would not she give me the purest of honey, the brownest of cakes, and the best of spruce?—and *does* not he give me the veriest dampers, made of bean-flour and bones, and the very sourest of swipes?" The Niss "paused for a reply," but as Eric could say nothing in defence of the miller, he said nothing at all, and the Niss continued. "Therefore, I say, she is too good for him, and he has had

her long enough. I thought that she would
have softened his heart and made him kind to
the poor, and that living with him would have
done her good too, and have made her humble
and amiable. But no! Jan would spoil anything;
and but for you she would have grown up as
wilful and spoilt at the mill as at court—Ahem!
Ak yaffo!—a—a—that is," resumed the Dwarf
in a great hurry, "but for you, Eric, she would
certainly have been spoilt, whereas now she
will be a blessing to all the country—that is,
round about here, round about here, of course.
And so Mr. Jan may whistle for his little Ethel
in a day or two; and then he had better look
out for himself, for he has been offending the
Grimm as well as me." And rising from his
seat, the Niss began slowly ascending the tree
again. He turned his head on his shoulder
when he reached the entrance to his hole, and
looking solemnly at Eric, said, "There'll be
the very dickens to pay at the mill shortly.
Bye, bye, my boy! My kind regards to your

good mother;—I won't forget her trees. Be a good lad and you will hear from me again soon;" and with another nod to Eric he crept into his hiding-place, pulling a large bunch of leaves down before it was lost to view.

Three days after this, led by the Prince Greatswello, with great sounding of horns and prancing of horses, a splendid cavalcade, accompanied by huntsmen and dogs and all that was necessary for hunting, appeared in the village. It fell to the luck of Hans to meet it before any one else, and by offering the good Prince such accommodation as his dwelling afforded, he so pleased him that he tasted bread and salt and drank milk under his roof, and when he left, told his Lord High Chamberlain to do something or other for him and his wife—a command which that functionary promised to obey, but, after the fashion of such persons, either "forgot to remember" or "remembered to forget."

Eric missed seeing the hunt. The goat

which he had trained for Ethel was lost, and on the day on which the visitors arrived he was away in the mountains looking for it. When, after finding it, he returned, the Prince and his followers had departed. Needless to say that a great state of excitement prevailed in the village after this unwonted event; and this increased when it was discovered upon the same evening that Ethel was missing. Great was the grief of the villagers, scarcely less great the wrath of the miller; and although this soon cooled down, he missed her so much that he offered a reward of two rix dollars (they were light ones which he could not change) for tidings of her. Far and near the country was scoured for days and days, but without any trace of her being discovered. When last seen she had been setting out for a walk in the forest, and at length it became the belief of the neighbours that, attracted by her beauty, the Trolls had spirited her away into Fairyland.

Poor Eric was in despair ; he had loved his playfellow fondly, and could not bear the thought of never seeing her again. Indeed, so much affected was he by his grief that he wore himself to skin and bone by fretting, and walked about as in a dream, a mere shadow of his former self. His parents began to grow very anxious about him, and talked of doctors and wise women. But Eric shook his head when they were spoken of, as if his sorrow was too deep to be cured by doctors and altogether beyond the vision of wise women, be they never so wise. Evidently the friendly Niss thought it wrong of him to trouble his father and mother in this fashion, for one day, when he passed under the birch-trees, he called out to him, and said—

"Don't be a donkey, Eric!" (Not very polite of him, perhaps, but then Nisses are exceptional people, and very plain spoken.) "Ethel is all right. The Trolls—confound them all for a set of noisy blacksmiths and

tinkers!—have not got her, and never shall
have her whilst I sit in this tree; so don't
worry yourself or your parents any longer.
Some day, when I think fit, you will see her
again. Don't look up; there is some one
coming! I am glad you gave that abominable
dog away to the miller, for I *can* get a nap
now without being disturbed by his howling.
As you are a good boy, and I knew that you
would not like to have him drowned, I did not
make him bite Jan; I made him bite the foreman instead, which rather pleased Jan than
otherwise. By the way, the miller's time is
growing short. He is going on at a fine rate!
My last cake from him was nothing but bones,
chips, and plaster; and as to the beer, it was
vinegar, and bad vinegar too! I made Tray
swallow it, and he yelped all night in consequence, and kept Jan awake. Ha! ha! ha!
Never mind, though; let him go on. You will
see some rare sport at the mill before long.
Go on now, and keep up your spirits! Ta ta!"

With a lightened heart (for he had full faith in the good offices of the Niss), Eric went on his way, resolving that the next cake he offered him should be of the finest flour the country could produce, and smothered in virgin honey.

CHAPTER III.

ONE day Jan Beanflaverem sat at his mill door—it was the day preceding that on which the people usually came in from the surrounding country to buy flour and meal, and as he was rather short of it the mill was rattling away merrily. Now the monotonous click of the mill had soothed Jan into a drowsy condition, and he felt very much inclined for a nap. " Clickety-clack, clickety-clack." Jan shut one eye. " Hum, hum, clickety-clack." Jan shut the other eye. " Burr, whirr, whur-r-r." Jan was almost asleep, when, a troop of boys playing by the river-side, and making, as boys will do when so engaged, a good deal of noise, awakened him. Considerably annoyed, he shouted to the children, and gave them bad words, ordering them to go away. For a time they were silent, but thinking, since they were not upon Jan's ground, that they had as much right to play as he to sleep, they presently recommenced.

"Clickety-clack, clickety-clack." Jan breathed hard, and his bright red nose, drooping towards his chest, looked as if it were on fire and about to burn a hole in his shirt front. "Clickety-clack, hum, whirr," went the mill, and "snore, snore, snort," went Jan, raising his head suddenly as a loud laugh from the children struck on his ear. Just at that moment one of the boys happened to shout again, and jumping up with a very wicked word upon his lips, Jan seized his stick and flung it at them. Unfortunately for him it missed them, and fell into the mill-head; and as they ran away laughing louder than ever now, he resumed his seat in a very ill-temper. The stick was ornamented with an ugly face, having two red stones for eyes at the end of it, and as the miller himself had carved it long ago, he grumbled and growled terribly at the loss of it. Gradually, however, the "clickety-clack, hum-m-m, whirr-r-r-r," of the mill soothed him again, and finally he slept soundly. A rude shake awaked him, and looking up he saw his foreman standing by him. The mill had ceased working.

"Hillo, Gaspar! Eh! Why, what have you stopped the mill for?" he cried in the greatest astonishment.

"That's what I've come to speak about, your honour," said the foreman. "None of us have stopped it; it has stopped of its own accord."

"Nonsense! you are playing tricks with me! Take care that I don't discharge you, sir, and get another foreman. Set the mill going again directly, you lazy dog! To-morrow is market-

"At length Gaspar chanced to look down between the mill-wheel and the wall."—*Page* 33.

day, and—aw-yaw "—(he yawned loudly as he
sank back in his chair)—"and we—aw-yaw—
must not be—yaw-aw—idle;" and he again
composed himself for slumber.

But the foreman insisted so earnestly that
none of them had stopped the mill, or were
able to set it going again, that, vowing vengeance against any and everybody, Jan rose to
see himself what was the matter. They went
upstairs, they went downstairs, they poked
their noses in here, they thrust their heads up
there, they pulled things about everywhere,
and from being mighty red in the face the
miller began to grow somewhat pale; but still
they remained as ignorant of the cause of
the stoppage as ever. Time went on; the
mill stood still, and Jan's prospect of profits
on the ensuing day was rapidly diminishing.
At length Gaspar chanced to look down
between the mill-wheel and the wall.

"I have it! That's it!" he cried joyfully.

"What?" inquired Jan, peering down also.

c

"That!—that stick there! It's jammed against the wall, and stops the wheel."

Sure enough there was a stick, at one end of which gleamed two little twinkling sparks. As Jan became accustomed to the light he discovered that the stick which was now stopping his machinery was actually the one which he had thrown at the boys in a rage. There it stuck, its red eyes winking and blinking at him in the dim light as maliciously and aggravatingly (so Jan thought) as possible. How were they to reach it?—and if they succeeded in doing so, how dislodge it? It occupied the only place where it could have had the effect of stopping the mill—the only place whence it was impossible to remove it without pulling down a part of the wall and sacrificing a week's work to repair it.

All this was extremely vexing to Jan, and not the less so because hitherto the machinery had always gone like clockwork, and had not caused him a moment's trouble.

" Ah, villain stick ! " he cried, shaking his fist at it, and oblivious that it was his own fault entirely that it had fallen into the river; "ah, villain stick, how I will cut you, and hack you, and slash you ! How I will bake you, and break you, and burn you when I get you out ! " And with a heavy heart he gave orders to pull down the wall.

When he recovered the stick he kept his word, and breaking it savagely into little bits, poked them into the fire. It might only have been his fancy, but he thought that he saw the red eyes blinking and winking and twinkling revengefully at him from the very heart of the fire long after the stick had been consumed. And so Jan lost his profits for a whole week, for the neighbours were obliged to procure their flour elsewhere.

Jan had lately taken to drinking, and grew more surly and morose every day. He had not a good word for any one. The very next week, disapproving of some beer which he had ordered a boy to bring him, he cursed and swore, and breaking the mug upon his head, some pieces of it (of the mug, not of the boy's head) fell over the coping of the bridge into the stream. That night Jan went to bed half tipsy.

About twelve o'clock he woke up. "Hey! halloo! Why, what's that noise?" he cried. "Some one has set the mill going!"

And sure enough it was so. The wheels were humming and whirring and clacking, the water rushing and splashing as usual, and it was all running to waste; there was not a sack of corn in the mill.

Jan jumped out of bed. "Run and turn the water off! Shut down the gate! There will not be a drop of water left by the morning!" he cried to two of his men, whilst he himself hurried on his clothes.

The men went, but returned declaring that with all their power they had been unable to force down the gate. Then Jan went with

them, and they all three tried to close the
hatch; but something had evidently got into
the woodwork slide, and they could not move
it. So the stream ran, and ran, and the mill
worked jovially to no purpose until morning,
when, the water having flowed away almost
entirely, and it being now quite light, they
were able to discover the cause of the obstruc-
tion. This proved to be a piece of crockery
ware which Jan recognised as part of the
mug he had broken the day before upon
the potboy's head. Sorry enough, and angry
enough he was too, for at least another two
days' work and another two days' profit was
lost to him. Moreover, his workmen became
gloomy, and whispered amongst themselves
strange stories of the pranks played upon bad
millers by the Grimm; the miller himself grew
frightened and superstitious; but he only drank
the harder and swore the more frequently, so
that in the end worse misfortunes befel him.

CHAPTER IV.

*HOW, WITHOUT PRACTISING, ERIC BECAME A
GREAT MUSICIAN.*

NOW Eric grew to be a very smart youth, and as good as he was smart. He was sprightly and gay, and he could dance, or wrestle, or shoot with crossbow or longbow better than any lad thereabouts. Besides understanding, too, all about flocks and herds, he could track and overcome wild beasts, and had killed both wolves and bears single-handed. Young maidens looked shyly at him, therefore, out of the corners of their eyes as he passed; but, true to the memory of Ethel, Eric cared for none of them.

At length his faith began to waver in the

promise of the Niss, and he was growing restless and discontented, when one day the Dwarf limped down the birch-tree and spoke to him.

"Ah!" he murmured, putting one of his legs tenderly to the ground. "I have a slight touch of rheumatism, my dear boy; a wet wren flew into the hole the other day. However, I suppose one must expect to ache a bit when one gets to be over a thousand."

"What! over a thousand years old, sir?" exclaimed Eric, opening his eyes; because really the Niss did not seem to be more than fifty or sixty.

"Precisely! Just that! Pull my leg, will you?" The little fellow extended his leg towards Eric, who handled it reverentially, but pulled it heartily. "Not so hard, confound you!" cried the Niss, for in Eric's hands the leg was absolutely expanding like a telescope or a piece of indiarubber. "That will do, . . . so, . . . h'm, that's better," and, released

by the young herdsman, the leg flew back to
its original size again.

" Now, young man!" exclaimed the Dwarf—
and by this time Eric *had* become a very fine
young man—" you have almost doubted me
lately."

" I am sure, sir, I never will in future,"
replied Eric apologetically.

" Don't," said the Niss sharply; " I don't
like it. You began to be afraid that you would
never see that young person who went away
from here just seven years ago, eh? Ah, I see
you did! You *do* wish to see her?" and pausing, he looked at Eric, who stood before him
in confusion, and at length replied in an almost
inaudible voice—

" Yes—yes—that is, if—if your worship sees
no objection."

"Ahem! Haw!" coughed the Dwarf grandly.
" How old are you?"

" Nineteen, sir."

" Nineteen! Dear me! what an infant!

Well, I suppose (for you imperfect creatures) that it *is* time for you to see her. H'm— h'm! There are difficulties. H'm. Let me see, now. Yes. I can only think of one way. You have a taste for music. I have heard your piping from my hole up there; it has given me a toothache often. But then, of course, you know nothing about it yet. Now my friend the Grimm, at Troll-Vracken Water- fall—whose cousin had been playing up 'Old Gooseberry' at the miller's of late—the Grimm, I say, is a superb performer—a master of the art—and can teach you in one lesson to excel on any and every musical instrument that exists. I will speak to him, and all that you will have to do will be to offer him a white kid. See that it is a fine fat one, or you may offend him; and cast it into that part of the fall which faces the north! The Grimm will then grasp your right hand, and thenceforward you will be able to play upon any instrument in such a way that everything will stand still, entranced, to listen, or will dance about or fall to fighting at your will. Above all, close your eyes when you make the offering, and do not look at the Grimm; and if you hear him playing when you approach, wait until he has finished. Afterwards say nothing to any one, but set out quietly to the Castle of Greatswello. You will easily find the way; travel eastwards towards the forest on the other side of the river at first. You will find her—never fear; and you have my orders to receive her."

"To receive her, sir?" ejaculated Eric in surprise.

"Receive her; yes. Don't I speak plainly enough. Ask no questions, but do as you are bidden. Any further instructions that may be necessary will be brought to you on the road by my messengers when I ⹀please. Meantime go to Troll-Vracken, and, by the way, both going and returning give the Troll-mounds a wide berth. Should you fall in with the Trolls, however, make for the rye-fields;

they cannot follow you there. Not a word; do as I bid you. And now good-bye, and good luck to you."

Eric after this was in a great state of excitement and delight at first; but when he considered where and among what grand people his pretty Ethel was, he became despondent. Even if he found her, would not her friends drive him, a poor herdsman, from the door? Nevertheless at the thought of the Niss he brightened up; the Niss, he felt sure, would not send him upon a fool's errand, and he determined to carry out literally the instructions he had received.

Saying nothing to any one, he chose the fattest and whitest kid from his flock, and waited in the greatest impatience for Thursday evening. It came. All day Eric had watched the sun until it was time for him to set out, and at length, taking the kid upon his shoulders and his tabor-pipe in his pocket, he started.

It was a long walk to Troll-Vracken fall, but

the young herdsman trudged along manfully.
The great pines rustled and rustled as the
wind swept through their lofty tops and died
away in a subdued roar miles and miles off in
the depths of the forest. As the sun drooped
lower Eric heard the bark of the wolf; but he
did not fear wolves (which at that time of year
were shy, and would not face a man); and even
if by accident he had come across one, had
he not his knife in his belt, and had he not
killed them single-handed before now? The
errand he was upon lent a sombre tone to his
thoughts. More than once he fancied that he
saw the red-crested Gertrude-bird—originally
a woman, who was turned into a bird for re-
fusing charity to our Lord and St. Peter—and
once he was convinced that he heard the
wild huntsmen in the distance; but the sounds
passed away. Still he strode onwards over
the silent carpet of dead pine-quills.

The evening darkened, the sun was setting,
when the far-off roar of a waterfall broke the

stillness. Now the forest grew thinner; birch-trees became intermingled with the huge pines; large ferns and grey boulders broke the monotony of the scene. As Eric drew nearer the din of rushing waters increased, and the shadows seemed to shift and quiver, giving the trees and rocks all kinds of strange appearances. Once or twice they looked so like huge and misshapen human beings, threatening him, that he shuddered and grew cold. But still he strode on courageously. And now a giant rock (which he knew was situated immediately above the fall) appeared in sight, and over it hung a light moving mist, twisting and writhing itself into a hundred fanciful forms, now dim and shadowy, and now dazzling with the last reflection of the setting sun. It was only the spray from the leaping water, and, nothing daunted, Eric gained the rock and climbed to its summit.

Below him lay a dark, troubled, foam-fleck pool of unknown depth; beside him rushed

the tremendous torrent. A rock in mid-stream
divided it, but the channel he overlooked fell
towards the north. The clause in his instructions which referred to this point was therefore
easily complied with, and he was turning his
head aside to cast the kid into the fall, when
suddenly the most ravishing music that mortal
ever heard fell upon his ears. It was the
Grimm playing. Chained to the spot, Eric listened intently, and with him all nature too was
hushed. The leaves ceased rustling, the ferns
stood still, the waters of the fall hung suspended, the birds became mute, and even the
hum of insect life was silenced. Tremulous
at first and low, the strain grew gradually into
a great burst of melody. Louder and louder
it swelled, until the very firmament seemed
filled with delicious sounds. Descending then,
and passing with wonderful facility through
various keys and changes, it seemed about to
die away, when it broke forth again, and soon
attained a power to be compared only with

" Lifting the kid aloft, he closed his eyes, and cast it far into the pool."—*Page* 49.

the thunder of a hundred of the largest organs. The rocks far and near resounded and took up the sound. Suddenly, in mid-air, it ceased, and for some minutes the surrounding air quivered and trembled, vibrated and rang with lingering echoes before all was still again. Then once more the trees began to rustle, the birds to sing, the insects to hum, the stiffened waters, released, dashed on their headlong course; and Eric remembered his errand, forgotten in the entrancement of the moment.

Lifting the kid aloft, he closed his eyes, and cast it far into the pool. Well, perhaps, was it for him that he had closed his eyes, for had he seen the awful jaws that emerged from the waters to receive his present it would have turned him into stone. Talk of teeth! Why there were rows of them, each tooth as long and sharp and crooked as a Turkish scimitar. And as for the mouth, it opened to such an extent that the tallest grenadier, with his bearskin on his head, might have walked into the

D

awful cavern without touching a tooth, as easily as he could have passed through the entrance of Drontheim Cathedral. But the eyes were the most terrible. They were as big as any ten lamps on a railway engine, and were formed of rings of different-coloured lurid flame, twirling and blazing fearfully. As for the Grimm's bristles and his horns, they were indescribable.

Keeping his eyes still closed and his head turned away, Eric heard the clash of those fearful jaws as they closed upon the fat little kid. Half a minute passed—it seemed half an hour; and what his feelings were in that time my young friends can hardly imagine. Presently he felt a sensation similar to that of a wet cloud enveloping him. Then his right hand was seized by what seemed to be the paw of a Polar bear; he heard the snap of claws, and was wildly tempted to open his eyes, but, fortunately restraining himself, felt one sharp squeeze, that appeared to press all his fingers into one; his arm was wrenched almost out of the socket, and then his hand was released. A few seconds afterwards he looked, and beheld nothing but the rapidly darkening prospect. His hand was hot; his arm ached; but fortunately for him the kid had been unexceptionable, and the Grimm was pleased; otherwise he might not have escaped so easily.

Eric descended from the rock. Night now came on swiftly; but, knowing his way thoroughly, he walked homewards by the glimpses of moonlight until he came to some open fields. Then for the first time he bethought him of his tabor-pipe, and putting it to his lips commenced to play. Delighted himself with the extraordinary tones he produced, he forgot the warning he had received from the Niss and passed near a Troll-mound. Out came the little Trolls in troops, in threes and fours, in tens and hundreds, swarming to the sound of his music, and, joining hands, they fell to dancing round the mound in the silvery moonlight. Round and round, faster and faster they flew, until the individuals that formed the ring could no longer be distinguished, and it looked like the flying wheel of some vast steam-engine.

Suddenly he ceased playing, and simultaneously they vanished from his sight; but at the same time a confused murmur of discontent and tiny threats arose. "Seize him! Bind him!" Thereupon Eric, becoming alarmed, and unwilling to be spirited away into Troll-land for the sake of his music, took to his heels and ran away. But the Trolls followed him. Faster and faster he heard them coming, although they were now invisible to him; and, anxious to learn how far a start he had of them, he turned his head upon his shoulder and put his pipe to his lips. Instantly he saw them close at his heels, and in his fears and endeavours to accelerate his speed he blew such harsh and discordant tones that his little

"Joining hands, they fell to dancing round the mound in the silvery moonlight."—*Page* 51.

enemies ceased running, and falling upon one another began to fight violently. But the instant Eric stopped playing the Trolls stopped fighting and recommenced their pursuit of him. So, playing and running alternately, he approached a rye-field, and remembering that the Niss had told him they were unable to follow through the stalks, he plunged into the rye, and soon left them behind. Fortunate for him was it that the Trolls had issued from the mound without their horses, or they would easily have overtaken him before he reached safety. As it was, he reached home safely, although much exhausted.

CHAPTER V.

JAN BEANFLAVEREM BECOMES A DRUNKARD—THE TERRIBLE CONSEQUENCES OF SEEING TWO PITCH-POTS.

NOW Jan Beanflaverem went from bad to worse. He was tipsy every day; his nose became as red as a strawberry, and he grew more sullen and morose than ever. Meanwhile the pranks played by the goblins terrified his workmen. Sometimes, without cause, the mill would stop suddenly; sometimes, with as little apparent reason, it would commence working when there was no corn to be ground and waste all the water; sometimes a great loss of time was entailed by the breaking of a cog or strap in the machinery. To compensate for being out of pocket by these misfortunes, Jan adulterated his meal and flour to such an extent that his customers could hardly eat it, and the consequence was, that they ceased to deal with him, and bought what they required elsewhere.

Mysterious knocking and rattling of chains were now heard about the mill, and at times, from deep down below its foundations, in the very bed of the river, the roar of supernatural laughter would rise above the splash and rattle of the wheel. Then one by one Jan's men began to leave him. But he did not care, not he! The more his fortune went against him the more wicked and obstinate he became and the harder he drank. He had no fear of goblins, nor of anything else, he said, for he did not believe in anything but himself and strong drink; and he vowed that, sooner than give in, he would stop and work the mill alone. Only let him catch one of those goblins or hobgoblins, and wouldn't he give him a nice warm black draught!

.. In view of this, knowing how goblins dislike pitch, he always kept the pitch-pot on the fire.

One evening, when the knocking and rattling of chains had been going on all day, the shrieks of demoniac mirth had been incessant; and even the machinery of the mill had played more extraordinary pranks than usual, the foreman (the last workman who remained) grew frightened, and told Jan that he would not stay there any longer. With threats and wicked words, the miller flung his wages at him, and he went away. Jan was left in the mill by himself.

Sitting down he began drinking, "to drown care," as he said, forgetting that it was drink and his evil ways that first brought care upon him. Glass followed glass, and after a while his spirits began to rise, and he sang and hallooed loudly. Presently he fancied that he saw two pitch-pots on the fire, and thinking, in his drunken humour, that one of the neighbours

was trying to boil a pitch-pot on his fire, determined to take it off and throw it into the river.

In his endeavour to move it, however (and
of course there was only one pot there, the
other being a mere drunken illusion), he upset
the pitch on the fire, and it rolled about the
floor in all directions in blazing streams.
Some of it splashed on his leg and severely
scorched him. Sobered by this, Jan rushed
out of the mill, bawling for help at the top
of his voice. But the neighbours had become
accustomed to his tipsy uproar, and no longer
took any notice of it; so that, before he could
make them believe that the mill really was on
fire, it was wrapped in great sheets of flame.
Some said that they saw strange goblin forms
running about it with torches, and setting light
to those parts of it which had not commenced
to burn. At anyrate, so rapid was the confla-
gration that it seemed as if some unnatural
power must have assisted it. Before night the
roof fell in; the big millstones thundered down

" Before he could make them believe that the mill was really on
fire, it was wrapped in great sheets of flames."—*Page* 58.

through the burnt floors into the river, sending
great showers of fiery flakes and sparks up to
the clouds, and the mill and all that it con-
tained was utterly consumed.

Now the report of Eric's wonderful skill as
a musician began to spread. With a penny
whistle he could make those people within
hearing of him foot it, and jig and hop like
peas in a hot shovel, until his music ceased,
and from the most cracked and battered of old
fiddles could produce tones that would draw
whole crowds after him, weeping, laughing, or
quarrelling, according to his will. He could
influence the beasts of the field too, or stop
the streams, and when he liked, cause even
the trees to cease rustling. Of course it was
whispered how he had obtained this power;
but the neighbours shook their heads, and
crossed themselves, and talked under their
breaths about it, for they knew that he had
the Niss for a friend, and were anxious not
to offend so powerful a personage.

Ruined as a miller, Jan Beanflaverem cast
about him for new means of gaining a live-
lihood, and hearing Eric play so beautifully,
thought that if he could only acquire the same
skill he would be able to travel about the
country and make a lot of money. Accordingly, in the course of a conversation about
Ethel, he wheedled the secret of the gift out of
the young herdsman, who always looked upon
him as Ethel's father, and could refuse him
nothing. Jan at once set about doing as Eric
had done. But, unfortunately, the kid that he
chose for an offering was a remarkably lean
one, which incensed the Grimm to such a
degree that when he seized Jan's hand he
squeezed it so roughly that the blood spirted
out from under his finger nails, and his arm
was sore for a week afterwards.

However, on his way home the miller thought
that he would have some fun with the Trolls,
and taking out a pipe with which he had provided himself, he began to play. The result

was not what he had expected. At the harsh tones he produced the little fellows rushed out in a rage, and falling upon him from all sides, kicked and beat him so severely that he was found half dead by the neighbours next day.

Repeated experiments proved to him that the musical power he had obtained only infuriated his hearers against him and brought him into trouble ; so finally he wandered away from the village one evening, and was never more seen or heard of. And what the end of the wicked miller was no one knows.

CHAPTER VI.

*HOW ERIC ARRESTED THE CURRENT OF A RIVER;
AND HOW HE AFTERWARDS CAMPED IN A
FOREST.*

IN the meantime, without saying a word
to any one, Eric set forth on his journey, with only an old violin at his back,
and his tabor-pipe, a crust of bread or two, and
some goat's milk cheese in his wallet. Turning
his face due east, he travelled for two whole
days. On the first night he found lodgings in
a herdsman's hut; on the second some gipsies,
charmed by the lively tunes he played them on
his pipe, gave him food and shelter, and were
very anxious that he should remain with them;
but he said that he was going upon an errand

which must not be delayed, and bidding them good-bye, set out again at sunrise. This was the third day of his travels, and he walked and walked until, about mid-day, he reached the banks of a broad and rapid river. Being rather tired and hungry, he sat down under a tree, and pulling out a crust of bread and cheese began munching it. But these remains of the provisions that he had brought from home with him were so dry that he was hardly able to bite them. At length, however, he finished his scanty repast, and rose and looked about him, to determine if possible in which direction lay his route.

Far and near no house or hut or sign of any human being was to be seen. It seemed as if he had gone beyond the habitations of man. Ten miles away on the other side of the river he saw a forest, beyond which blue mountains marked the horizon, and he thought, if he could reach the borders of the forest before nightfall, that he might find some woodcutter's

E

hut there. But the river was deep, and too
rapid for him to venture to swim across it, and
as far as he could see up and down its course,
there was nothing like a bridge or boat of any
kind to help him. Still, having come so far, he
did not like to turn back.

In his perplexity he sat down again, mechani-
cally fingering the strings of his violin, which
of late had become rather a habit with him
when in thought. The theme he chanced upon
in the few notes he struck interested him, and
bringing his bow to bear upon the instrument,
he launched into a bolder strain, creating at
length a maze of entrancing melody. As the
air grew wilder and wilder, though yet more
sweet and beautiful in its tones, the speed of
the current before him appeared to diminish.
Slower and slower it waxed, and slower still, till
at length it stopped altogether, arrested by the
music. Now when Eric saw this a thought
struck him; and rising quickly, without ceasing
to play, he walked down the banks. As he

had expected, he came to a spot where the river was dry; for, having continued to flow where it was beyond the influence of his performance, it had run away altogether below a certain point.

Before the young herdsman lay the dry watercourse, strewn by all manner of strange things. Amphibious monsters and odd fish danced and flung themselves about in all directions, and it was not without some misapprehension that he glanced at the dark wall of water suspended above him, and only held in check by the spell of his music. Nevertheless he began his passage across, and had almost reached the opposite bank when he saw a fine salmon in his path. It occurred to him that it would make an admirable dinner, so, stooping suddenly, he seized it by the tail and flung it on to the bank. But a mishap now befell him, which, in his eagerness to provide himself with food, had been overlooked. The instant he ceased to play, down came the waters in one huge wave,

"He had almost reached the opposite bank when he saw a fine salmon
in his path."—*Page 67.*

rolling over and over him. Fortunately his
proximity to the bank enabled him to grasp
the bough of an overhanging tree, and dripping
wet through, but otherwise (save that he had
lost the bow of his violin, which was swept
away by the stream), none the worse for his
immersion, he pulled himself on shore.

As the sun was shining brightly, he took off
his clothes and spread them out to dry. Meanwhile he took possession of his salmon, and
having knocked it upon the head, cleaned it,
and cut it in slices. Then collecting a quantity
of dry wood and sticks, which he heaped over
a couple of flat stones, he procured some rotten
touchwood from beneath the bark of a decayed
tree, and setting light to it with a flint and the
back of his knife, soon had his fuel in a blaze.
When it had burnt long enough for his purpose,
he laid bare the flat stones, now quite hot, and
covering them with salmon steaks, swept some
embers over these, and allowed them to cook
gradually. By-and-by he took out the steaks,

blew the dust from them, and putting some of
them in his wallet for future consumption, made
a splendid meal off the others. His clothes
were now dry, so he dressed himself and continued his journey.

Onward and onward he marched, over a
rude plain dotted with juniper-bushes. It
was much farther to the forest than he had
anticipated, but he kept up his spirits and
persevered. Afternoon began to wear away,
whilst he had still some distance to go; evening came nearer and nearer, and just as the
sun was getting low, weary and way-worn, he
reached the thin outskirts of the woods. Here
he paused and looked about him. There was
no cottage or hut of any description in sight.
What was to be done? The night, which
in these regions comes on very suddenly,
would soon be upon him, and to enter the
forest at such an hour would only ensure
losing his way. Moreover, it would soon
become bitterly cold, and it was necessary to

kindle a fire, not only for his own comfort, but to keep off the wild beasts which might otherwise molest him. He determined, therefore, to stay where he was.

Hard by he found a spot where a few thick juniper-bushes and a gigantic boulder of rock (from the base of which trickled a tiny rivulet) afforded a snug shelter from the cold wind. Having gathered some armfuls of withered fern, and spread it thickly for a couch, he got together a pile of broken wood and sticks, and had barely lit his fire when the night closed round him. The cold slices of salmon warmed over the embers afforded him a good supper, and when he had finished it he sat basking in the blaze of his logs, wondering how and when he should reach Greatswello Castle, whether the Niss would keep his promise to send directions to him as to what he was to do; and if he did do so, how he would send them, and how find him out so far away from home. As he mused thus, under the comforting warmth of the flames, he began to nod; soon he became too drowsy even to think; so, heaping fresh wood upon his fire, he said his prayers, coiled himself up in his nest of fern, and fell asleep.

· CHAPTER VII.

HOW ERIC WAS CAPTURED BY ROBBERS, AND HOW HE ESCAPED FROM THEIR STRONGHOLD.

BEFORE long he was roused by a rude blow, and frightened that he was in the clutches of some wild animal, he scrambled at once to his feet. The stars were shining brightly, and by their light he saw a tall savage-looking man, with unkempt hair and ragged clothes, leaning upon a long crossbow, and gazing at the fire.

"Who art thou?" he asked, raising his dull leaden eyes to the young herdsman's face.

Eric answered that he was a poor minstrel journeying to the Castle of Greatswello, and that he had been benighted on the road.

"Hillo, comrade! Thunder and lightning, whom have you here?" he asked.

"Only a minstrel lad, who has lost his way in the forest, and who wants a night's shelter," replied Eric's companion. "Show him the way down, Gustar."

"A night's lodging! H'm. Thunder and lightning! A night's lodging, eh? Well, get in with you, youngster;" and pointing to a rope ladder similar to the one outside, he motioned to Eric to descend.

Down, down, down, into the bowels of the earth he went. Thirty-five rounds of the ladder had he counted as he ascended, but now he counted fifty-two before his foot reached solid ground. It was quite dark then, for the small hole above was obstructed by the two men, who, after interchanging a few words and drawing up the outside ladder, followed Eric, carefully closing the trap-door behind them. When they also had reached the ground, one of them advanced; the click of a latch was heard, and a light burst on them from an open door. In the room, now revealed, Eric saw a third man reclining upon a rude settle before a fire, the smoke from which was carried aloft by a pipe. He rose to a sitting posture as they entered, and glared savagely at the new-comer.

"How now, Gustar! Are we to have all the world in our secrets?"

"'Tis only a youth in place of little Kenneth," returned Eric's captor; "he had lost his way in the forest, and I found him asleep. I thought he would do to cook, and wash plates, and so I brought him with me. Did I not right?"

"Right? By the hammer of Thor, you did wrong! By the Great Serpent of the Midgard, you are a dolt and an idiot to bring a stranger into our stronghold!"

"Ho! ho! If you have any fear, it is easy to silence him;" and he passed his hand across his own throat in a way that, as plainly as possible, indicated a proposal to cut Eric's.

"Say the word, and it's done," he said, drawing a long knife from his boot.

"Well, well, we'll see about it; there is no hurry; we can see what he is good for first. It is easy enough to slit his weasand or knock him on the poll at any time; meanwhile he is safe enough here. By Loki, our patron, people don't get out of this place very easily! No, no!" And laughing gruffly, he threw himself back upon the bench on which he rested.

Eric now knew for certain that they were robbers, and not the Prince's foresters, that he had fallen amongst. At the words of Gustar he had quietly grasped the handle of his knife, determined to sell his life dearly; but since there appeared to be no immediate intention of harming him, he grew calm again, and sitting down on a log of wood, looked more closely at his companions.

Three heavy-browed, ragged-haired, blear-eyed villains they were, such as I trust it may never be the lot of any of my young friends to

meet in wood or copse when they play truant
from school. Upon their heads were huge
broad-brimmed hats; round their waists broad
black belts, furnished with tremendous brass
buckles; and their great brown boots were
like enormous fire-buckets. Their beards stuck
out all sorts of ways like brambles, and their
moustaches were like the very largest cork-
screws. The seams of old wounds scarred
them all over. One had a long patch of
sticking-plaister across the bridge of his nose,
another a patch from eye to jaw, and the third
had a big patch somewhere else. As to their
knives, and daggers, and swords, and bows
and arrows, and I don't know what else—
clubs, and all sorts of battle-axes, most likely
—they were a terrible sight to see. Neither of
the robbers could speak three words without
swearing horribly, drinking deeply, smoking
determinedly, and frowning fiercely. They
were indeed most terrible fellows.

The den they lived in was furnished with

three settles, and had one cupboard. The
earth, beaten hard, formed the floor, and the
main beams of the roof were some of the
largest roots of the tree above. One flaring
torch of pine-knots was stuck in the wall, and
the place was half filled with smoke, which the
rude chimney but imperfectly carried off. It
was a wretched abode; and little wonder was
it that Eric's spirits fell as he looked around
him and reflected on his position.

"Thunder and lightning! get supper, boy!"
cried the second robber, pointing to the cupboard.

The poor lad rose, and soon laid before his
masters an enormous ham-bone, a cold pie, a
great loaf of black bread, an immense mustard-
pot, holding pints and pints of mustard, and a
soup-tureen full of cayenne pepper. Then
from a corner he took a large earthen pitcher
full of fiery spirits of some sort; and the
robbers began to eat. They swallowed the
mustard and pepper in mouthfuls, and they

drank and drank the fiery spirits until the pitcher was empty. When it was filled again they recommenced drinking. And so, laughing, and swearing, and quarrelling, and making friends again, they prolonged the orgy far into the night.

All poor Eric's thoughts were directed now towards escaping, for he expected every minute that, in a sudden fit of passion, they would fall upon and kill him. He looked at the door ; he thought of the rope ladder. But the three robbers were between him and this means of exit, and for the present he wisely pretended, therefore, to have submitted quietly to his fate. Nevertheless he felt very miserable when he remembered his parents and the beautiful Ethel, from whom it seemed that he was now cut off for ever.

Presently the chief robber cried, " You said, Gustar, that the boy was a minstrel ; let's have some music—a song with a chorus ! By Thor's hammer and the Midgard serpent, we

F

will!—we'll have a rousing chorus and wake
the night! Play up, boy, play up!"

"Play up!" they all shouted together.

"But, gentlemen, I have lost the bow to
my violin, and I cannot play without one," he
protested.

At this they were so furious that they
threatened to kill, ay, and eat him too, if he
did not play at once. But suddenly one of
them remembered that they had an old bow
somewhere, which had belonged to some poor
traveller they had murdered, and after a little
search he found and gave it to Eric. As he
played they sang, and growing quite delighted
with his music, they shouted out chorus after
chorus in drunken glee. He changed the tune
to a quick and lively measure, and joining hands
they danced to it, laughing immoderately, until,
by degrees, as they were growing tired, he
played slower and slower, in a way that had a
sleepy, dreamy sort of effect upon them. They
left off dancing, and sat down; they began

nodding slowly to the tune, their eyes closed, their chins drooped upon their chests, and at length they fell fast asleep.

When Eric saw this he rose up, and, still playing softly, edged towards the door. Not without difficulty he managed to open it with his elbow, and groped his way to the ladder. But he found that to ascend he should require the use of his hands, so he was obliged to cease playing. The robbers, however, were snoring loudly, and he began to climb as quickly as he could. He had completed half the distance when he heard one of them move; an exclamation ensued, and redoubling his exertions, he had just reached the top of the ladder, and was seeking the bolt of the trap (which, to his horror, he found was some secret contrivance), when one of the men came out of the room with a firebrand in his hand. Holding it aloft, he discovered Eric, and with a loud oath and a shout to his companions, he roared to the lad to come, or they would make mince-meat of

him; at the same time he took hold of the
ladder, and almost shook him off it. But at
this moment, by good luck, he touched the
secret spring, and the trap-door flew open.
The other robbers had now appeared; whilst
he who had given the alarm had begun to scale
the ladder, and was already within a few feet
of the top. Eric sprang on to the platform.
But even if he got away from the tree, the
robbers would now be in full chase of him.
His only chance of escape, therefore, lay in
destroying the ladder. Drawing his knife
hastily, he slashed the side ropes of it across.
Beneath the heavy weight they bore they
gave way immediately, and with a tremendous
crash his pursuer fell to earth again. Almost
immediately two crossbow bolts flew through
the trap, one of which shaved the sleeve of
Eric's doublet. But he closed the door, and
dropping the outer ladder, rapidly descended
to earth. Then, fearing that the robbers might
have some other means of exit from their den,

he hastened to conceal himself in the densest part of the thicket, where he paused and listened for a moment. But all was quiet; he heard nothing; and, thankful for his wonderful escape, he continued his journey by the dim light that now and then broke through the tree-tops. At length, quite worn out by the night's adventure, he climbed into a large ivy-grown tree, and finding a safe perch there, fell fast asleep.

CHAPTER VIII.

A CONVERSATIONAL JACKDAW—A MESSAGE FROM THE NISS—A MOMENTOUS ENCOUNTER—THE CAPTURE OF THE ROBBERS.

AT daybreak Eric woke, and descended from the tree, feeling stiff and cold, owing to the cramped quarters he had occupied. There was a little brook close by, and after washing his hands and face, he ate his last slice of salmon and crust of bread, and began to consider seriously how he was to continue his journey. For some time he wandered on rather aimlessly, and at length came to a place where four narrow paths met. Here his perplexity increased. Which path should he follow? If he took the wrong one, it might lead him back to the robbers—a con-

tingency he dreaded to contemplate. Oh that
the kindly Niss, who had promised to advise
him, would only send him some hint now !

"Halloo!" cried some one near.

He looked all round, but could see no one.

"Halloo!" repeated the voice in a somewhat
harsh tone.

Again Eric looked about him, but was still
unable to discern any one.

"Halloo!" he heard a third time.

The voice seemed to come from above, and
glancing up, he saw, seated on the branch of
a tree, an old grey-headed Jackdaw. And a
most comical figure he was. Round his neck
was an old cambric frill, and sticking upright
from his tail were two peacock feathers, of
which he seemed very proud.

He looked at Eric, and Eric looked at him.

"Halloo, you, sir!" said he in a hoarse,
croaking voice (that was not very intelligible,
for, although jackdaws *do* speak, they cannot
express themselves very clearly). "Do you

mean to say that fine feathers don't make fine
birds?" and he turned round slowly, as pea-
cocks and turkeys do when displaying their
plumage, and, shaking his tail, made his two
false feathers quiver in so queer a fashion,
that Eric was like to die of laughing. Fortunately the Jackdaw's back was turned to him.
" Do you mean to say that fine feathers *don't*
make fine birds, eh?" he repeated, giving his
tail a wag and a jerk, that nearly set the
young herdsman off again, and had the effect
also of making one of the feathers drop and
hang loosely downwards. ". Drat that feather!"
said the Jackdaw, scratching his poll with his
claw in vexation; "do what I will, it won't
keep up. Look here, my fine fellow; now
I tell you what it is, if you can only manage
to make that feather stick up as it ought to
do, I'll do you a good turn."

" Very well, sir; I will see what I can do;"
replied Eric; "but you must fly down here
first of all."

"Do you mean to say that fine feathers *don't* make fine birds?"—*Page* 88.

"Fly down there, must I? Not a bit of it. If I did I might lose the other one. No, no, my lad, you must climb up to me."

This was rather a tough job; but having walked round the tree, Eric found a practicable spot, and began to ascend. In his pocket he happened to have some string and a piece of wire, such as his mother used to tie down the corks of her spruce beer, and with these he did not doubt that he should be able to afford his new acquaintance satisfactory assistance. He soon reached the branch upon which the bird was perched, and seating himself astride of it, produced the necessary articles. The Jackdaw turned his tail towards him, and whilst he worked, continued to twist and turn his head about, as a vain old woman in the hands of her maid or dressmaker might do.

"Now, be careful, sir," said he; "take care that you do it right, and see that it sticks up straight—mind! Do you hear?"

"Yes, sir—ma'am," replied Eric in perplexity, for he really did not know which term was correct.

"Ma'am!" ejaculated the Jackdaw in high dudgeon. "What do you mean by that? How can a *Jack*daw be a ma'am?"

"I beg pardon, sir; it was my mistake."

"I should rather think it was; you don't suppose it was mine, do you?"

"No, sir; certainly not. But you must tell me if I hurt you."

"If you do I'll bite you; and if I do bite you, you will remember it," said the bird viciously.

Taking hold of the stump of the daw's tail, Eric twisted the wire two or three times round it, being careful not to do so too tightly. "Does that hurt you?" he inquired.

"Not a bit; you can give it another half turn if you like." Eric did so, and the Jackdaw started. "I was very nearly biting you that time. Don't do it any tighter."

"No, sir; that is quite as tight as it need

be." Parting the two ends of the wire until they stood up like a V, Eric layed the stump of a feather along each of them, and securely fastened it with string. They stuck up now famously, and firmly enough to allow their being shaken to any extent. " There ! " said he, " that's capital !"

" Yes," answered the Jackdaw, " I can feel that that's capital. They do spread nicely. They won't come undone, will they ? "

" They won't come undone till the string wears out, and that will be a long time."

It occurred to Eric that in one of his pockets he had a little crushed doll's hat that he had plaited of rushes for Ethel years and years ago. His mother had put a small feather in it and decked it with a pink ribbon, and a few days before he had set out it had chanced to turn up among some other trifles of Ethel's which he had taken possession of. To be sure, it was crushed and rather dilapidated, but he soon poked it into shape again.

"What's that?" asked the Jackdaw, eyeing it curiously.

"A pretty little hat, sir; and I thought, as it is rather cool at night, that you would not object, perhaps, to accept it."

"It *is* a very pretty little hat, and it is cool of a night. Put it on for me."

Eric did so, with some difficulty concealing his mirth. "There now, it looks quite charming."

"I daresay it does; but you haven't such a thing as a looking-glass about you, have you?"

"No, sir, I am sorry to say I have not."

"Idiot!" ejaculated the Jackdaw. "How am I to see it, then?"

"Well, sir, there's a clear glassy pool of water close by; you could see it in that."

"So I could," returned the bird, brightening up. "But if I flew to it, I might disarrange my costume. Look here! I will sit on your shoulder, and you can take me to it, and then put me up here again."

With the Jackdaw upon his shoulder, Eric
carefully descended the tree and walked to the
pool, where he placed him upon the bank.
Here he stared at his reflection in the water,
and turned, and strutted, and twisted himself
about in such a way that the young herdsman
had the greatest difficulty in restraining a
regular outburst of laughter.

"Now take me back again," he said at
length. And when he was once more upon
Eric's shoulder he asked triumphantly, "And
now, do you mean to say that fine feathers
don't make fine birds?"

"Not at all, sir; I never thought of such a
thing. You are a fine bird."

"You think so?"

"Certainly, sir—a very fine bird."

"Very fine, eh?"

"Very fine indeed,—quite splendid, in
fact."

"You don't say so! Dear me! You are
very polite;" and the Jackdaw bridled, and

quivered with delight. "Well, now, I have a message for you."

"For me, sir?"

"Yes; a message for you, sir. I have been expecting you for hours and hours."

"How did you get it, sir?"

"From a grasshopper—a green and golden grasshopper. I had picked him up, and was just going to eat him, when a most dreadful stitch in the side forced me to drop him. And would you believe it, he sat up on end and spoke to me! I never was so astonished in my life; for, though we daws speak just as well as you do—in fact better, since we excel you in grammar, pronunciation, and expression— yet grasshoppers! The impudence! However, in a kind of whistling squeak, he certainly did give me a message for you; so there is no mistake about it."

"And the message, sir?"

"Well—let me see—it was a sort of rhyme. How did it go? Oh, he sang it. I'll sing it too." And putting himself into an absurd attitude, he croaked—

> "Take the path to the east,
> And the path to the west;
> The north to the Bear,
> And the south to the Nest,
> So shalt thou prosper, pros—per.

"There! What do you think of my voice? Don't I modulate nicely? Ah, you should hear me shake!—you shall when I've had a little more practice. But that's your message —great nonsense it seemed to me; perhaps you understand such gibberish, though, better than I do."

While the Jackdaw was chanting the above lines, it seemed to Eric that hundreds of tiny voices took up the notes at the word "prosper," and looking round, he fancied that he saw scores of little fairy faces peeping at him from out of every flower and from beneath every leaf. But they soon vanished; the chorus

G

ceased, and nothing was to be heard but the rustling of leaves, the hum of bees, and the morning song of birds. So, thanking the Jackdaw, and bidding him farewell, he continued his journey, taking the path which ran towards the sun.

Thicker and thicker grew the forest, black, desolate, and inexpressibly dreary; still Eric pressed on, breaking twigs and branches from time to time, in order, if necessary, to be able to retrace his steps to the four cross-paths. As he walked along he repeated the rude rhyme chanted by the daw, partly to fix it in his memory, and partly because it puzzled him. All that he could make of it was that at first he was to follow the path to the east; and he had no doubt that circumstances would arrange the rest. After walking for some hours the forest began to clear; he passed through an open glade or two, and at length emerged into a fair and cultivated country. Whilst he stood surveying it a horseman approached. He was armed with sword and dagger, a ponderous mace hung at his saddle-bow, and his three armed attendants (one of whom carried his lance) proved that he was a knight of some renown.

"Good morrow, fair sir," said Eric, politely doffing his cap as the stranger came up.

"Good save you, friend," answered the knight, a man of middle age and grave and commanding presence, and reining in his horse he looked steadily at Eric.

"Can you inform me, sir, how far I am from the Castle of Greatswello, and which is the way there?"

At this the stranger murmured softly to himself, "It is he," and without answering Eric's question, asked in turn what his business might be at the Castle.

But the lad had already gained sufficient experience not to tell his affairs to every one he met, and therefore answered, "Courteous sir, forgive me if I answer that my business is of a private nature, and I must be excused from exposing it."

"Truly, truly. As thou wilt, young sir. Thine own courtesy reminds me that I was wrong to ask the question. Forgive me. I return to the Castle myself shortly, and will gladly show you the way, if it please you first to bear me company a space. I am bound upon an enterprise in which I am led to think that you can assist me. It is neither more nor less than the capture of three villains, outlaws and robbers, who infest this forest, and who have plundered many travellers hereabouts, and even murdered some. Parties of armed men have often been sent after them; but some of them have disappeared altogether, and others have suddenly lost all trace of the robbers in deep dells and tangled thickets; so that hitherto they have escaped. I have now taken a solemn vow to capture them, and I must fulfil that vow, or ever remain man-sworn."

Doubting not the identity of the robbers, Eric related all that had befallen him (saying nothing, however, of the manner in which he had put the thieves to sleep), and offered to conduct the party to their den.

"Now Heaven be thanked for this auspicious meeting!" exclaimed the stranger. "If you can do this, doubtless we shall be able to destroy them and break up their stronghold. Then shall I be relieved of my oath; the plunder we find in their possession shall be yours, the whole country will have cause to be grateful to you, and well I wot that the Prince Greatswello himself will refuse you nothing."

With a cheerful face Eric assured him that he could make good his offer; and calling one of his attendants (whom he addressed as Fritz), the knight told him what Eric had related to him, and asked his opinion about it.

"So please your worship," said Fritz, "these are probably the very scoundrels that we are in search of; and if the young man can re-

member the road, I will wager that we render
a good account of them."

Mounted behind Fritz, Eric led the way back
without difficulty, owing to the broken twigs and
branches with which he had marked his course,
and about noon they reached the spot where
the four paths crossed.   Here the young herdsman looked round for the Jackdaw; but he
was no longer to be seen, and having rested
for a little, and partaken of some provisions
produced by one of the squires from a large
wallet, they proceeded.

The path to the east had conducted Eric
to the stranger, thus giving him the means
of an introduction to Greatswello Castle; the
path to the west was of course the same path
retraversed; so, following it up without hesita-
tion, he soon reached the tree in which he had
slept.   Thenceforward the track was harder
to find; at times they lost it completely, and
had to dismount and search all round about
to recover it.   They persevered, however, and

finally Eric saw before him, in the midst of a
tangled thicket, the robber's tree. On coming
up to it, they found that the rope ladder still
hung from the outside, as Eric had left it.
It seemed, therefore, probable that the villains were prisoners in their den. And so
it proved.

Followed by the knight, Eric mounted the
ladder. Their first task was to destroy the
trap-door, which only opened from within;
and this, after some labour, they accomplished.
As the last fragment of it fell into the tree,
three arrows whizzed by them, one passing
through the young herdsman's hat, and another
grazing his shoulder. Evidently the robbers
intended to defend themselves, and the question now arose, How were they to be got
out? A variety of plans were discussed; and
at length Eric's proposal " to smoke them out,"
as he had often done wild animals when hunting, was adopted. Accordingly large faggots
of greenwood were collected, kindled, and

lowered into the tree, the hole at the top
being then carefully closed; and after a while
the inmates called for quarter. On condition
that they surrendered their arms and gave
themselves up as prisoners (in which case, at
Eric's intercession, the punishment of death
was commuted for perpetual banishment to
the mines), it was granted to them. A rope
was lowered, to which they attached their
weapons; and after these had been secured
the ladder was drawn up and readjusted, and
finally the robbers themselves, wretched, crest-
fallen, and half suffocated, came up one by
one, and were severally pinioned.

Each squire now took one before him on
horseback, whilst Eric mounted behind their
leader; and leaving the case for examination
on a future day, they worked their way back
to the cross-paths, and thence to the open
plain again. Arrived there, they dismounted
and held counsel together, at the conclusion
of which the three squires remounted, and,

taking the robbers with them, rode away in the direction whence they had first come, and were soon lost to sight. Eric was left alone with the stranger, and was wondering how all this might end, when, pausing in front of him, the latter said—

"Good youth, thou hast rendered me a great service. Heaven, through thee, has favoured me exceedingly, seeing that without loss of life or limb we have relieved the country of the bandits who have so long troubled it. I have sent my companions to lodge them safely in our dungeons at Greatswello. But I have yet another task upon hand, and one, I warn thee, of greater difficulty and moment than the last. As I cannot well undertake it without an attendant, and as I have seen in thee coolness, discretion, and address beyond thine years, I have chosen thee to accompany and aid me with thy counsel. If thou likest to undertake the expedition, and we succeed, I am sure that thy claims upon the Prince

will be sufficient to ensure his granting thee
anything to which thou mayest aspire. My
intention is, if possible, to capture or destroy
the great bear of the Dovrefeld, a monster
that has long ravaged the districts on this side
of the mountains, and has slain and carried
off to his den innumerable men, women, and
children, keeping the country side in mourning
for years."

At the name of this dreaded monster, the
fame of whose exploits had even reached the
little village he had left, Eric was astounded.
It seemed incredible that one man should dare
to undertake a task in which, as he well knew,
large parties had often failed, and for some
moments he remained in thought. By degrees,
however, the difficulties began to vanish in his
mind; his confidence returned, and looking
up, he boldly announced his resolve to accompany the Knight, adding that he doubted not
in the least that they would be able to overcome the beast if they could only find him.

"That," said the Knight, "is my chief difficulty. No one has ever been able to track him to his den, and I know not how to proceed."

"'The north to the bear;' that is clear enough," said Eric to himself. "I know not, Sir Knight, whether I can of certainty conduct you to it, but I have faith in my good genius, and will try. I can but fail; in which case we are no further from the accomplishment of your design than we are at present."

"You speak well and wisely," replied the Knight. "Lead on; I will follow you. Bring me to the den of this monster, and if I slay him, anything that I have shall be yours."

"It seems to me, Sir Knight, that, since the afternoon is wearing on and we may have far to go, it would be well to wait until the morrow, when, being well rested, we can start early upon our adventure, with the whole day before us."

"You counsel well. Yonder is a deserted

woodcutter's hut, where we shall doubtless find what we require."

Accordingly they entered the hut, and lighting a fire, supped heartily off some provisions which the squires had left with them, and in due course, recommending themselves to God, lay down and went to sleep.

CHAPTER IX.

HOW ERIC KILLS THE GREAT BEAR, AND ARRIVES AT GREATSWELLO CASTLE.

EXT morning early, when our two adventurers set out, Eric led the way to the junction of the four paths, and choosing the one which pointed northwards, followed it closely. After a toilsome march they emerged from the forest, and saw before them a chain of wild and lofty mountains, apparently inaccessible, and rendered dangerously slippery by the torrents that poured from rock to rock, moistening everything with their drifting spray.

"From the descriptions given by huntsmen who have followed the beast, this seems to be the very spot where they have so often lost sight of him," said the Knight. "Yonder, too, is the swamp, in attempting to cross which more than one has lost his life." He pointed as he spoke to a stretch of bright green verdure near them, beneath the thin surface of which lay black slimy mud of unknown depth. Beyond this was what appeared to be an insurmountable precipice, and turning away, the Knight said, " Evidently we cannot pass here; and if we could, the precipice would stop us."

But the path, albeit barely distinguishable now, still ran towards the quagmire, and Eric replied, " Nevertheless, Sir Knight, it is in this direction that our course lies, and if I mistake not, we shall have to cross this swamp."

Dismounting, therefore, the Knight tied his horse to a tree, and he and his companion made their way slowly to the edge of the swamp, where all traces of the path finally disappeared.

"Chee-cheek, chee-cheek," chirped some-thing close to Eric's ear, and looking round, he saw seated upon his shoulder a large green and golden grasshopper with diamond eyes. As it peered into his face, with its head screwed round and its slender legs out-stretched, it had a comical appearance, which somehow reminded him of his old friend the Niss. "Chee-cheek," chirped the grasshop-per again; and though to others it would have had no meaning, to Eric it sounded like "Follow me." At this moment the insect jumped from his shoulder on to the swamp, and after turning round and cocking its head in a knowing fashion, sprang another yard in the same direction.

Now all this was very surprising to the young herdsman. From the odd likeness of the grasshopper to the Niss, he did not doubt that it was the messenger from whom the Jackdaw had received his message, and he concluded that it had now come to render

him further assistance. Testing with a stick
the spot of ground to which he had leapt, he
found that, owing to a foundation of roots or
decayed wood, it was tolerably firm. With
a sharp "chee-cheek," as if angry at being
doubted, his guide hopped another yard into
the swamp. Here, too, Eric found firm
ground, and enjoining the Knight to follow
carefully in his footsteps, by noting each time
where the insect alighted, he led the way
safely across the bog. Here the grasshopper
left them.

Path there was now none. Before them
rose the precipice, and since it was impossible
to pass round it, they had evidently to sur-
mount it. After carefully surveying it Eric
began the ascent, and little by little, taking
advantage of every reft, or ledge, or tuft of
grass that afforded support, scrambled higher
and higher, followed by the Knight, until,
hanging upon the side of the cliffs, they looked
like flies upon the side of an enormous plum-

cake. After many a dangerous slip and much arduous toil they reached the top. But it proved to be only a bare ridge of broken rock. At their feet lay a narrow gorge, black and tremendously steep. A mist came up from it perpetually, and the faint noise of waters that ran far, far down below, might be heard from time to time. Near them were the roots of a fallen pine, the upper branches of which rested on the far side of the ravine. And here for the first time traces of the bear were seen. With great delight Eric pointed out the marks of his claws upon the bark, which proved that he was in the habit of crossing the tree ; and seating himself astride of it, he gradually worked his way to the other side of the ravine, his companion doing likewise. The bear's tracks were now clearly distinguishable, and in a very short time they stood before the cavernous entrance to his rocky den.

All around were strewn bones, fragments of armour, and shreds of various habiliments all blood-stained and rather worn. Here and there the gaunt and sombre boulders bore quaint resemblances to wild animals of monstrous size, and had a gruesome look. Altogether it was an eerie spot.

Upon carefully examining the ground, they found a small hole above the cave, and on listening, plainly heard the bear moving below them. Eric's hunter-craft now stood him in stead. Gathering together a heap of sticks, he bound them into a faggot, and setting light to it, said—

"Now, Sir Knight, stand you over the mouth of the cave whilst I drop this faggot through the hole. And when the bear rushes out strike him full on the nose, so haply you may kill him."

With his heavy mace poised over his shoulder and his sword and dagger ready, the Knight then took his position above the entrance of the cave, and Eric dropped the blazing pine-faggot into it. A terrific growl followed, and the next moment, with roars that made the crags re-echo and were fierce enough to appal the stoutest heart, out rushed the bear. He was a fearful monster, ten times larger and a hundred times more ferocious than any bear you ever saw in the Zoological or any other gardens. For. fifty years he had ravaged the country, and, as you may suppose, had grown to an enormous size in that time ; whilst the number of human beings that he had eaten easily accounted for his unusual savageness.

As he issued from the den the Knight aimed a tremendous blów at his nose, which is a bear's most vulnerable point. But the monster was too quick for him; he only fell on his haunches, and turning with jaws extended, he attacked his enemy furiously. By the exercise of great agility the Knight avoided him, and striking and thrusting with his sword, wounded him in several places, so that he appeared to be having the best of the combat. Fortune, however, deserted him, for, stepping back hastily, he slipped upon a loose stone, and before he could recover himself the bear was upon him. Seizing him between his horrible paws, which could easily have crushed an ox, and rending his coat of fine chain-mail as though it had been some silken fabric, the animal raised himself upon his hind legs, and lifting his victim off his feet, hugged him closer and closer, until, under the dreadful pressure, he fainted. In another moment the Knight's head would have disappeared between Bruin's great foam-flecked jaws. But just at this critical juncture, when it seemed that nothing could possibly save his life, Eric drew forth his pipe and commenced playing a quick, sprightly tune.

At the sound of the first note the bear turned his head, relaxing his crushing grasp upon the Knight; and Eric, knowing, as we all do, how fond bears are of dancing, blew away louder, and quicker, and more merrily

"Stepping back hastily, he slipped upon a loose stone, and before he
could recover himself the bear was upon him."—*Page* 116.

than ever. The bear let go the Knight, and, forgetting all about the combat, began shaking his head and jumping about on his huge hinder paws, turning and wheeling in a way so uncouth and ludicrous that, despite the fate of the poor Knight and the danger he himself was in, Eric was like to split his sides with laughter. As he played, drawn irresistibly by the music, the bear came nearer and nearer; and seeing that he was regardless of everything but his style in dancing, Eric drew his knife, and still piping as the monster came jigging towards him, took deadly aim, and plunged it to the hilt into his eye and brain. With a last faint hop and a kick, he fell down and died, moving his head and shaking his paws to the tune that had so fatally absorbed him.

Eric now ran to his companion, whose face he bathed with some water from a hollow in the rock, and who after a while, uttering a deep sigh, came back to life, and asked what

had become of the bear. The young herdsman told him that he had slain him. Presently they went to the spot where he lay, and,
overjoyed at his death, and at his own merciful
escape, the Knight thanked Heaven devoutly.
Though he could not quite understand how
it had befallen, for Eric had not disclosed
to him the secret of his marvellous musical
powers, nevertheless he felt that he owed him
his life, and he was proportionately grateful.

Cutting off the bear's head and paws as
trophies, they set out to retrace their steps.
Soon they reached the fallen pine, and without
mishap descended the precipice and recrossed
the swamp, their track through which Eric had
taken the precaution to mark with shreds of
bark stripped from the stick he was carrying
when the grasshopper first appeared. Mount-
ing the Knight's horse, which was found where
they had left it, they rode back into the forest,
and having at length reached the cross-paths
again, paused a little to consider.

The Knight was in favour of taking the track they had before travelled, and so issuing quickly from the wood. Mindful, however, of the directions conveyed in the Jackdaw's rhyme, and remembering that by following them implicitly they had prospered hitherto beyond all expectation in their undertakings, Eric besought him to go instead by the southern route.

"But," protested the Knight, "why should we go that way when this, I am well assured, is the nearest to the Castle. Yester morn thou askedst me the road to the Castle and the distance there, and I promised to guide *thee* thither; now thou wouldst guide *me*. The path thou pointest to goes no one knows whither. To what end is this fancy?"

"I know not, Sir Knight," responded Eric; "I only know that my good genius bids me take this direction, and sure I am that there is reason for it. I beseech you, come with me, for I must travel this way, whether thou

followest it or no; and if you do not, evil will
certainly befall you."

"Prithee lead on then, good youth. So far
thou hast been fortunate indeed, and I cannot
part from thee. Be it as thou wilt."

Taking the last of the four paths, therefore,
Eric strode manfully on. It was a long and
weary scramble, and weakened by the wounds
he had received in his struggle with the bear,
the good Knight could hardly keep the saddle,
and was forced to relinquish the bridle to his
young guide. More than once, when they
found themselves at fault and had to halt to
make out the track, he blamed himself for
yielding to what seemed to him his companion's folly. But, undismayed, Eric strode
on in silence. By a sorely hard and difficult
ascent they came at length to the summit of
a mountain chain, where the forest terminated
abruptly. At their feet lay a fertile valley, on
either side of which rose lofty hills, bare and
ragged-crested, but the lower slopes of which

were clothed with pines; and immediately below them, upon a spur of the mountain on which they stood, was a magnificent castle, which the Knight recognised at once as Greatswello.

. "Hadst thou taken my advice we should have been there four long hours ago," he said.

"Nevertheless," replied Eric, "rest assured that what has happened is for the best. What may yon ivy-clad tower that stands so gracefully apart from the rest be called?"

. "That is the Dove's Nest," answered the Knight, glancing round sharply and scrutinisingly at the querist. "There the Prince's daughter dwells when it is her pleasure to seek retirement."

"His daughter!" echoed Eric carelessly. "If rumour speak truly, she should be no less fair than good."

. "Beautiful indeed is she. But this is passing strange," murmured the Knight to himself;

"I cannot fathom it. Let us descend," he continued aloud; "afternoon grows apace."

Slowly they descended to the Castle, Eric musing the while upon the name of the ivy-clad tower.

"The Dove's Nest! Can that be 'the Nest?' —'the south to the Nest.' And yet I cannot understand—'the Prince's daughter.' Ah, I see it! The Princess has taken a fancy to Ethel, and retains her among her maidens. Yes, that must be how it is, and I shall see her again at last! Oh, happy, happy day!" And, satisfied with this solution, he strode gaily down, nor paused until they stood before the drawbridge of the Castle.

As they approached the warder blew a resounding blast upon his horn, and the gates flew open quickly; whilst, with every symptom of respect and consideration, the guard turned out and saluted the Knight.

Thought Eric to himself, "My companion is evidently an officer of consequence in the

Prince's service, and I am lucky to have fallen in with him."

Two gorgeously arrayed pages now advanced, bowing deferentially, and after a few words in an undertone with one of them, the Knight gave Eric into his charge, and bidding him farewell for the present, passed through a little doorway and left him.

CHAPTER X.

WHEREIN IT IS SEEN, THAT ALL THOSE WITH WHOM WE ARE CONCERNED LIVE HAPPILY EVER AFTER.

THE young page showed Eric into a comfortable chamber, the magnificence of which, unused as he was to anything of the sort, astonished him. Such curtains, fringes, canopies, settees, such furniture and appliances, such dresses and accoutrements, as he now saw he had never before dreamt of. Of course his companion was accustomed to them, and he noticed his surprise rather contemptuously, being especially amused when Eric started at his own vivid reflection in a mirror of burnished steel. It was a pretty thing, thought he, that he, Alberic Fritzperbelow Tweedledee, should have to attend upon a vulgar fellow of this kind. When the young herdsman asked, therefore, the name of the Knight who had brought him thither, he answered pertly—

"We call him Sir Caspar. And you, what do they call you when you are at home, eh?"

Although the tone of the question brought the colour into Eric's face, he was too proud to attempt to conceal his humble origin, and he answered simply and honestly, " I am the son of Hans the herdsman, and my name is Eric, the son of Hans."

At this piece of intelligence the young fellow's nose turned up with a sniff, and he tried hard to twist his moustachios, but as the hairs were only about as long as those on a mouse's tail, he did not succeed very well. The other page, Almaric Fitzfardingal Foodledoo, joined him presently, and *his* nose turned up so, after they had conversed a little, that you would have thought it never by

any possibility could recover its usual shape.
They both questioned Eric now, asking him
how the cows were, whether cheese was
plentiful, and so forth. By-and-by, however,
they left him; and as he sat down at the
casement, and looked out over the strange
land before him, he felt sad and lonely, and
almost wished that he had not left his home.
Determined, though, not to betray his mortifi-
cation before strangers, he subdued it, and set
to work, with the washing apparatus that he
found at hand, to remove the travel-stains
and dust from his person and clothes. These
last were rather better than were usually worn
by persons in his station, for his mother, who
was very proud of him, had made them of
the best and smartest materials that she could
procure. Being a tall handsome youth, his
picturesque garb became him amazingly, and
when he had completed his preparations, his
appearance left very little to be desired.

Upon resuming his seat at the casement, he
aw a party of soldiers that had set out from

the Castle soon after his arrival riding hastily back to it with several prisoners, bound and pinioned, amongst them. There was a great stir presently in the court-yard below, loud talking and exclamations of indignation and surprise, and shortly afterwards Sir Caspar himself strode into the room where Eric was.

" I owe thee much, young Eric," he said gravely and kindly ; " indeed I have only just learnt the extent to which I really am indebted to thee. I promised that anything in my possession should be thine if I succeeded in ridding the country of that hideous monster of the mountains. The Prince has charged me to tell thee that he holds himself likewise bound to thee. But thou hast delivered me from a fate worse even than death, for since our conflict with the bear thou hast preserved me from a life-long captivity. An hour ago I despatched a troop of soldiers to ransack the robbers' den ; and as they wended thither they came upon the rear of a party in ambush, under the command

I

of my deadliest foe, who had intended to capture me as I returned home.   Taken in rear and at a disadvantage, the force was thoroughly defeated, and amongst the prisoners made is the man who laid this trap for me.   But for the determination not to return by that road I must have fallen into it; and so I am indebted to thee both for life and freedom.   Now, touching thyself: I have seen in thee a rare combination of courage, firmness, shrewdness, and discretion. Thou art fitted for great stations.   I would fain secure thee for the Prince's service.   How can we tempt thee?   Dost thou desire wealth?"

"No, Sir Caspar, but little wealth will serve my turn," replied Eric modestly.   "Enough to supply the wants of my dear parents in their old age is all that I require."

"Thou speakest wisely," said Sir Caspar with a deep sigh.   "Well, what *is* thy desire? Hast thou ambition?   Wouldst thou have rank —renown—power?"

"No, no," replied Eric, who was thinking of

Ethel, " I care for none of these; they would but ill become me." ·

A look of pain stole over the Knight's face. " Thou must stay with us, at all hazards," he murmured.

" My errand done, Sir Knight, I must return to my parents."

" Not so. Listen. I have an only daughter," he said in a troubled voice, "and she is beautiful and good; I—I cannot part with her." He paused.

Eric was almost as troubled as Sir Caspar. It was all very strange, he thought. What had he to do with the Knight's daughter? At length he said, " I thank you, Sir Caspar, for any kindness, of whatever kind it may be, that you may wish to do me, but my object in seeking the Castle of Greatswello was to find a little girl—a young woman, I mean—who—I——" He stopped in confusion.

" And so, Sir Herdsman, you refuse the honour of my daughter's hand!" exclaimed

Sir Caspar, frowning heavily. "A fine tale to be told, truly!"

"Nay, indeed, Sir Knight, I meant no disrespect whatever. You are very kind—far, far kinder than I deserve; and your daugther may be lovelier than all other maidens on the earth, whilst the offers of service that you make me might well tempt another. But let me remind you that I am only a poor herdsman; these honours would not become me, and instead of making me happy, would only create me enemies. If I can only find the maiden that I seek among the tire-women at court, I will, God willing, go back to my home, and rest contented with whatever Heaven may please to send me."

"Thou art wrong, Eric. Honours become those of noble heart and nature, and such I deem thou art. Birth none of us can command. A turn of the wheel of fortune, and I might have been the herdsman, thou the Knight. Of what we make ourselves we alone have the right to be proud. Pride of birth, alas! too often engenders indolence and folly, although, rightly felt and worn, it may restrain us from mean and cowardly actions. Had I fifty daughters, I would rather wed them to such as thou, who would raise up a race to do honour to their ancestry rather than draw honour from it, than give them to the butterfly popinjays at court, whose descendants would resemble themselves. I can see far enough into the future to know that times are coming when wisdom and great deeds will outweigh the accident of birth. Think again, then, before you refuse."

"Sir Caspar, it is useless," answered Eric. "I feel your kindness deeply, but Ethel is dearer to me than all the world besides."

"Ha, ha! Sayest thou so!" replied the Knight, a merry twinkle in his eye belying now the gravity of his countenance. "There is a rival, then. So, so, this is serious. My daughter shall hear thy refusal from thine own lips."

"How, Sir!" quoth Eric, shocked beyond measure at the proposition. "Pray, do not so

cruel and ungenerous a thing;" and he hung
back as, grasping his wrist, Sir Caspar was
drawing him from the room.

"Permit me to know best what is cruel and
ungenerous, young sir, I am unused to beg,"
replied Sir Caspar sharply.

"I could not say aught to wound your
daughter's feelings, but yet I——"

"Thou mayest trust me not to outrage my
daughter's feelings, methinks. Come! follow
me!"

And, not knowing how to refuse him further,
albeit still determined to wed no one save her
that he loved, Eric obeyed.

At the end of a long and lofty corridor was
an archway, masked by drawn curtains of heavy
drapery, fringed massively with gold, which, as
they approached, two pages (with silver wands,
and very large rosettes on their very little
shoes) respectfully drew back. A blaze of light
burst upon them; they entered; and, looking
round, Eric found himself in a great hall,

crowded by graceful ladies, gorgeously dressed,
stern soldierly men in rich attire, elderly digni-
taries in powdered wigs and long robes, and
glittering courtiers, bowing and cringing as only
courtiers can bow and cringe.

The hum of conversation ceased upon Sir
Caspar's appearance, and with a sweeping bow
to all he proceeded to the other end of the hall,
and seating himself in a great carved chair
upon a daïs, beckoned to the young herdsman
to approach.

His consternation and amazement may be
realised when he found that Sir Caspar was
none other than the Prince of Greatswello
himself!

In his rough garments Eric certainly looked
very much out of place amidst so much magnificence. Nevertheless, since he felt that he
had done nothing to be ashamed of, he held up
his head, and with firm step and erect carriage
walked boldly through the brilliant assembly.

The Prince whispered a few words to a

page, and after a short delay, during which Eric
gazed curiously on the scene around him, a stir
amongst the ladies at hand attracted him, and
a silvery voice, that thrilled him with delight,
asked musically—

"Did you send for me, my father?"

Eric turned. Advancing towards them was
a young maiden of surpassing beauty, and at
that moment her glance fell upon his face.

"Ethel!"

"Eric!"

She halted, and both stood still in the greatest
perturbation and confusion.

It was indeed the little Ethel grown into a
lovely and graceful woman.

The Prince looked on with a smile; but the
courtiers, shocked beyond measure at hearing
the Princess thus familiarly addressed by a
simple herdsman, thought that the end of the
world could not be far distant.

"Well, my good Eric, what sayest thou
now?" asked the Prince laughingly.

"Ah, Sir, you overpower me with your goodness!"

"Goodness! Where should I now be but for thee? My bones would be whitening in the desolate mountains, or I should be hopelessly imprisoned in a castle dungeon. Besides, I can never allow my daughter to die an old maid and the line of Greatswello to become extinct, which she threatens shall come to pass. Eh, puss? Have I found the right suitor for thee at last? Have I discovered the reason why the young Count of——? But, there, I will say no more.

"And now, ladies and gentlemen, the surprise upon your faces reminds me that some little explanation may be welcome, perhaps, to you. Seven years ago I was, as you know, a childless man; and being strangely drawn towards this fair maiden by her resemblance to one now with the saints, I adopted her. She was then a little prattler of ten years old; but my heart ached with the void caused by the loss of my only daughter and the simultaneous death of her mother, and I thought perchance that she would help me a little to forget. It were needless to remind you how kindly and fondly she has always treated me. How I became possessed of her you never knew. During one of my hunting expeditions I had become separated from my attendants in the chase, and was seeking a convenient spot to rest me in the forest, when I found, asleep upon a bed of moss, beneath some shady boughs, the loveliest little maiden that I had ever seen, save one perchance. As I have said, no child's voice lightened my leisure hours, no gentle offices of love from affectionate hands soothed the passage of my life or promised to temper the loneliness of my old age; and as I gazed at this fair waif a great longing sprang up within me to call her mine. Half inclined to bear her away with me, I was standing there irresolutely when a noise in the tree above attracted me, and looking up, I saw a very remarkable little old man—a

" I found, asleep upon a bed of moss, beneath some shady boughs, the
loveliest little maiden that I had ever seen, save one."—*Page* 138.

dwarf oddly dressed in grey hose and a peak cap. 'Why don't you take her, Prince?' he asked. 'Nay, how can I take her when she is not mine?' 'But suppose that you have as good a right to her as any one else—supposing that I give her to you, how then?' 'Have you the right to, sir?' I asked respectfully, for somehow this little man, who looked so young, and yet so old and wise, impressed me with reverence. 'I am the Niss, Prince, and I give her to you; that is enough,' he said. 'Fear not, she is mortal, and a kind, loving little thing to boot. But'—and he shook his long, long forefinger impressively—'I only give her to you for seven years, mind! At the end of that time I shall require you to deliver her into the hands of him that I shall send for her, and woe betide you if you strive to evade this condition.' You all know the power for good and evil that the Niss possesses, and upon these terms I joyfully accepted his gift. Lately forgetful, of the compact, in my schemes for the Princess's welfare, I have allowed many nobles and men of merit and valour to seek her hand. All these she has steadily refused to listen to; and a message which I received, no matter how, a week or two ago dispelled my projects by announcing the immediate termination of my agreement with the Niss. I was further advised to undertake the enterprises which you have just seen successfully concluded, and warned that the envoy to whom I was to deliver my daughter would be sent to me in the character of an assistant. The deep obligations that I am under to this youth resolved me to endeavour to attach him to my service by offering him my daughter's hand; but he has refused all my advances, and since no such contingency as this was provided for in my compact with the Niss, I am gravely perplexed."

He paused, and the Grand Chamberlain, a pompous old dignitary with a tremendous wig and a wonderful air of self-satisfaction and stolidity, shook his head wisely, and with such vigour that the vast clouds of powder from his hair set several of his immediate neighbours off sneezing.

"Ahem! Good my Lord, we know nought of this youth's lineage, education, or fortune. Judging—ahem!—by appearances—though " —(and this was uttered mighty oracularly)— "appearances are sometimes deceitful—ahem! —why—ah—why—haw—yaw—I should say that—er—he is somewhat—eh ?" And he looked to one of the pages who stood near him with his nose still turned up, to supply him with an epithet.

"Seedy," suggested the page contemptuously.

"He looks, as my young friend here observes——" continued the Chamberlain.

"Ask your young friend to step through that doorway to the head steward's office, and ask the head steward for his wages, and then ask your young friend to pack up his traps and march out of the Castle in double quick time. And as for you yourself, old Powder-puff, when you are told by your master to do something handsome for a deserving herds-man, you remember to do it, and don't re-member to forget it, or you will very soon follow your young friend, I can tell you," said a shrill voice from behind the Prince; and looking in that direction, they all saw, seated cross-legged upon the topmost orna-ment of the back of his carved chair (though how he got there no one could tell), a little old man in a red peak cap and a grey worsted dress. "I can answer old Powder-puff's question myself," continued the Niss, looking at the Grand Chamberlain without the least particle of reverence or respect—a proceeding to which that awful functionary was by no means accustomed. "The youth's lineage is in the highest degree respectable, and quite as ancient as that of any one here. He is descended in a direct line from Adam. You may judge of his education by his actions and

" Looking in that direction, they all saw, seated cross-legged upon the topmost
ornament of the back of his carved chair (though how he got there no one could
tell), a little old man in a red peak cap and a grey worsted dress."--*Page* 144.

K

bearing. As for his fortune, why, all the
spoil found in the robbers' cave, besides the
large rewards offered for their capture and for
the destruction of the bear, belongs to him;
and I can see the soldiers returning now with
three large bushel-baskets full of jewels and
gold. How many bushel-basketsful can you
boast of, old Powder-puff?

"And now, Eric, a word in your ear. Burn
your pipe, and give up fiddling, except upon
rare occasions, or bad luck may befall you.

"Ha, ha, ha! ho, ho, ho! You positively
stopped the river above Trollvracken the other
day, and my good friend the Grimm found
himself rolling about in a dry bed, as helpless
as a stranded porpoise. He has not suffered
such an indignity since the day that the gods
fished Loki out of the waterfall—hundreds of
years ago. Ha, ha, ha! What a day that
was, to be sure! By the way, my old tree
has been blown down; so, as there are some
snug corners in the ivy about 'the Nest,' I

have resolved to emigrate here. Take care
that no one interferes with my quarters, or I
will play the very mischief with the dairy.

"Good day, Prince; you have kept your
word like a man, and it is not every one who
does that now-a-days, or the world would be
a world the better and happier for it. Live,
and be happy in your daughter's union—if
there is any happiness in having a swarm of
sturdy, noisy brats springing up around you.
Ah! by the way, a word in *your* ear too.
Ethel *is* your daughter. You remember the
flood that washed away that part of the Castle
in which your infant child was asleep? Well,
that flood was presided over by a friend of
mine whom you had offended. (Take care
how you speak disrespectfully of the water-
sprites in future.) I interceded for you, but
all that I could obtain permission to do was
to steer your daughter's cradle safely down to
Jan Beanflaverem's mill. Jan took it in, and
the child and the jewels as well;—he was

always taking in something or somebody. Here's the cradle; I saved it at the fire. Goodness knows what became of the jewels." As he spoke he drew from his pouch a tiny berceannette, not larger than a child's shoe, and descending from his position on the chair, placed it upon the floor, where it rapidly grew and expanded, until it became a really good-sized cradle, which the Prince, of course, recognised immediately. (Who would not recognise the cradle that his infant occupied only seventeen years before?) "If you still doubt her identity," continued the Niss, "you may assure yourself of it by the mark of that flea in the Lord Chamberlain's ear—it was there a few minutes ago, Chamberlain, wasn't it, eh?" and he looked at the astonished functionary with a malicious grin ;—"you can't have forgotten it. Say, then, are the proofs legal and satisfactory, or do you require others?"

"Quite satisfactory—quite, quite so—surperfluously so, in fact," replied the Chamberlain, frightened out of his usual air of measured deliberation, and speaking more hastily than he had done for forty years past. " Nothing could be more strictly legal, your Worship— I mean, my Lord,—that is, your Reverence; there could not be a doubt as to the validity of the proofs—not a shadow of a doubt."

"Very good. Then all is as, it should be; so, ta-ta, Eric;" and with a smacking kiss, that resounded through the hall like a pistol-shot, upon the lips of the blushing Ethel, he bade a fair farewell to all this goodlie companie.

THE END.

PRINTED BY BALLANTYNE, HANSON AND CO.
EDINBURGH AND LONDON.

CPSIA information can be obtained
at www.ICGtesting.com
Printed in the USA
BVHW051817191218
535985BV00012B/221/P